MILK ROUND

Andrew George

LIVE CANON

First Published in 2015
By Live Canon Ltd
www.livecanon.co.uk

978-1-909703-09-4

Edited by Helen Eastman for Live Canon
www.livecanon.co.uk

MILK ROUND

Andrew George was born and raised in London. Following a spell as a voluntary support worker with the London Borough of Islington's sensory impairment team, he read English at Oxford University where he served as the student newspaper gossip columnist and the Producer of the annual touring comedy sketch show, 'The Oxford Revue'. Andrew qualified as a barrister in 1997 and has since practiced law at London's Blackstone Chambers specialising in commercial, financial services and media and entertainment law. He has regularly been involved in litigation arising out of international conflict and cross-border political disputes involving, amongst others, entities and individuals from Russia, Iraq and Libya, and has acted in many of the highest-profile cases arising out of the 2008 financial crash. He was appointed Queen's Counsel in 2015. Since 2008, he has also been Chairman of Trustees at the East End charity, Spitalfields City Farm, which conducts outreach work and on-site horticultural projects in the heart of London's Tower Hamlets. Andrew's poems have appeared in many leading magazines and journals, including *Magma* and *The Rialto*. This is his first collection of poetry.

Acknowledgments

The following poems have been previously published in the following journals:

'Careers Day', 'Dubrovnik', 'Smoke Without Fire', 'Ohio', 'Shark (Juvenile)' in *Magma*; 'What the Intern Meant' in *Octopus*; 'Mentor', 'Bang! Crash! Wallop!' in *Quantum Leap*; 'Milk Round' in *Poetry Nottingham International*; 'Hopping On', 'Testing Time' in *The Rialto*; 'Windfarm, Agrigento' in *Oxford Poetry*; 'Cape Cross', 'Parting', 'Lament' in *Envoi*; 'The Internationale' in *The Shop*; 'Circle Line' in *The Interpreter's House*; 'Diagnosis Day, New York' in the Philip Larkin Society & East Riding Poetry Prize Publication.

With grateful thanks to Tamar Yoseloff and Helen Eastman.

Contents

MILK ROUND

Andrew George

For Sara and Athene

Careers Day

Props are good. The soldiers bring their guns.
Helpful if the kids get out of hand.
This bloke I knew at school has got this look
'So you and whose – bleep – army. Mine's right here.'
The surgeon has his instruments on show.

The vet has brought a rabbit. I am with
a lawyer from a water firm. His speech
is rather dry. (The children don't laugh either,
faces blank with unallotted future).
Use the wig and gown. Give them the old

razzle-dazzle. *So who has been in Court?*
Most of you. *And why was that?* A range
of relatively trivial offences.
What do you think of barristers? I see.
I'm sure he did his best to get you off.

We do need some material to work with.
And on we flog. Fair punishment, perhaps.
We grew up here. We also smirked and scoffed.
An actress begs, *Just don't end up in Tesco.*
She's followed by a manager from Tesco.

Teacher, bring this torture to an end.
So now who knows what job they want? It seems
they all want to be comedians.
I know some good comedians. They're so
serious when they talk about their work.

What the Intern Meant

1. She routinely used a pilcrow. She was a certified sommelier, perfumer and Arabic translator; creative in her use of equitable doctrines. She said when she was President of college, and working in a strip club to pay her way through law school, she had to join the feminist protesters every night, then find a time to slip in through the back and start her shift. She would not base a case on an estoppel by convention. She worked in media for years and, they said, had parallel affairs with a talk-show host, a drummer and a minor politician. I could not bring myself to google this. She could recognise a trustee de son tort.

2. She left before she showed me how to find it. Now, if I should cross-refer to what I said before, I open up a piece of her old prose, then copy, drag and gently paste her symbol into my unfinished train of thought (see ¶1 above).

Salaryman

The tea's gone cold, of course. That highlighter
will not survive the hours its spent untopped.
The shock, though, is his stapler, jammed and wrenched
apart so that it splays across his desk.
He hated things like that – his hole punch
emptied every night, his bulldogs filed by size.

He must have got an email as he worked,
strapped into his tie and cancelled lunch,
practised looking earnest in the lift
and thought *Why me? My figures aren't so bad.*
I'm careful with my 'Internet research'.
I said sorry to the Swedish cleaner.

Here's a baseball cap with this firm's logo,
a golf umbrella branded by the client,
a mousepad crammed with pictures of his daughter,
and this must be a photo of his wife,
tucked into the lowest corner, balanced
under shelves of rainbow lever arches.

They'd de-activate his pass before
he left, 'escort' him out the fire door,
then let it shudder-slam against the wall.
He'd try to act unflustered on the street,
stroll towards the tube or buy a sandwich
as if he might yet eat it at his desk,

but here's the Swedish cleaner with a bin bag
gathering the personal effects.
She tosses in the brolly, cap and mousepad,
quickly overlooks the dusty wife,
extricates the staples and reloads,
then adds the punch and clips, which he would miss.

Mentor

So these grey hairs have earned the right to write,
this old corroded liver rated wise
enough, long after the event, to speak
of how it is along the beaten track.
Well, someone has to break the news to you.

I've passed the police records check, won't give
away my surname, mention sex, must guide
you, teenage mentee, to a path by which
you can descend in safety to the core.
A citizen to make the city proud.

Such flotsam and such jetsam as have stuck
and might congeal to flame a greasy lamp,
I give this willingly to you – for all
tomorrow's interviews and tests –
those bleeding-knuckle bouts you'll have to fight,

and if I have some sense of how to laugh
it off, or find the strength to stagger up
again, or best conceal an open wound,
if I have learned to turn a trick or two,
perhaps these words could be some use to you.

For though I am no goddess in disguise,
and cannot shield you from the waiting blows
or grant your prayer upon a sudden whim,
your arrows seem as sharp as anyone's.
Now launch them on this unsuspecting world.

Milk Round

How expertly you bit each canapé
and swallowed hard, and touched your bottom lip
with that soft tongue, then picked the punchline up.
I watched you captivate the sweating room.
They swarmed like nervous addicts for their fix.
It's fifteen years ago this evening, Kate,
and all the tyrants are retired or dead.
The students here tonight were toddlers then.
Your heavy laughter scatterbombs the room.
The prawn tempura circulates again.
You're halfway through a favourite anecdote.
The children do not know how it will end.

Bang! Crash! Wallop!

Like timpani that roll to a crescendo,
the gossip surges as you cross the room.
The higher-minded person's sweeter strain
is drowned by this reverberating beat.
Each champagne flute just resonates with news
of how and where and who did what to whom.
I sense you willing me to turn the tide,
but there are things I have to learn and things
I must correct about the episode
we know took place last night. The symbols clash.
We don't know the conclusions to be drawn.
You are the only topic for discussion.
You made your bed; we know who lay in it.
Now listen to the rising repercussions.

'... though neither virgin nor upper class ...'

I absorb your cheerful parting text,
can almost see you cross the business lounge,
perfect nails now tapping your last post,
graceful unringed fingers easing back
some Montrachet or maybe Albarino,
slivers of sashimi by your side,
headed to your old New World for good.

Grown weary of your fabulous career,
you said the time had come to pack us in
and so you checked through thirty years of baggage.
You thought you might exceed your 'single limit'
but all you found you had were souvenirs –
a lifted Tower Bridge, a cruising taxi;
your men as light as Christmas decorations,
carry-ons for you to take on board.

Now you must be ready to take off.
I think you'll take a little chilled champagne.
Perhaps a smile is softening the creases
that crept across those huge pacific eyes.
You'll settle back to feel the sharp ascent –
nose arcing firmly at the sun,
drifts of punctured clouds beneath your feet.

Smoke Without Fire

Slanted rain,
satisfying crease of
cellophane.
Dig the seam.

Forget friends first.
Grab your own.

The last match sighs
and dies.
Back inside
the music mocks –
light up, light up.

As if you had a choice.
You beg to
strangers.

And now you are ablaze.
On the one hand, you wave your little sparkler like a wand,
on the other hand, huge inclusive gestures,

in between,
a slight breath-
                    lessness.

The Oral Tradition

There's no bonfire in this city pub.
We huddle round the raconteur for warmth.
Another year of new recruits to share
the hoarded gossip, indoctrinate with legend.
The family is comfortably seated,
so once the Brewer's Gold is poured, the Guinness
settled, when the Zinfandel's uncorked,
and all the nuts are open, we'll begin.

The first stories are the safest – low
comedies, all binge-a-thons and pratslips.
Then the epics – Michael's fall, the fighting
until the final ousting of the old guard.
The gentle later bottles bring the love talk –
the decades long on-off office romance,
affairs that you can only say in whispers,
the gorgeous child of an uncertain father.

Here I might tell a joke against myself
or trace the punchline from a favourite fable.
A generation since I first took arms,
downed the sweetening nectar and became
a member of this ancient story-circle.
Performers pass away, their words remain,
and where I cannot recollect events
I still remember how they told the tale.

Fleet

The world's pressed on. Only the comics remain,
some religious periodicals,
an odd Sunday paper that's popular
in Glasgow, old art deco fixtures, and every
other door a tired half-lit pub.
There is no hack to file the breaking story,
no stringer with an urgent scoop to tout,
no editor to hold a whole edition.
People scurry into outfitters,
cut sharply through the paralysing chuggers,
stare thoughtfully at skinny macchiatos,
and jauntily evade the tourists setting
up their shots of phone-boxes and taxis.
Some tip-tap intensely on their tablets,
thrust their lives into the sticky web.
Others let their stories stay unshared,
as the river underneath this street
flows swiftly, undiscerned and undisturbed.

Model Village

The principal attractions are the trains
(showing off their points, their lines, their whistles,
steaming out of sleepy country stations,
sticking to their closely printed schedules),
hydrofoils that skate across a sea,
precision-scaled conveyors in the smelter.
But I prefer to count the model people,
freed from all their daily helter-skelter,
frozen, like some party game command
unlifed these clingy children, burdened mothers,
red-cheeked men with half-drunk pints in hand.
There's one bloke by the swings who holds his lover
rapturously, as if he might have chosen
to stop the world forever at this moment.

Hopping On

I ride the famous tourist bus for hours,
learning how to grip the metal handrail
as we corner, where to duck my head
beneath the scratch of overhanging branches.
I've crossed this 'fine example of Rococo
engineering' several dozen times,
then passed the Jewish cemetery, the Imax,
the papal chateau and the crazy golf.
These gravely bearded men still shoot their cards.
That overheated couple on the bench
lick the wounds they gave themselves this morning.
The herd of children drilled into this school
at half-past-eight are avalanching home.
Things suddenly accelerate unwisely.
A district is demolished, then a smallish
war begins and ends, a baby reaches
breeding age and founds a dynasty
that waxes proud and falls to insurrection.
I've started to distrust the placid voice
telling me to hop off where I want.

Wind Farm, Agrigento

Amongst the crumbled hypostilic temples,
six travellers are searching for a guide.
Across the entrance, orders have been hoisted,
All visitors must leave no childs behind.
Above, the giant snow-bright turbines turn,
calm amid the clamour, like a God,
the mystery of the twirling three-winged cross,
silent and extravagant and good.
The tour guide from the future drops his voice:
And these? The later ancient people built
them. Just before their energy ran out.

Dubrovnik

We could make love. The heaving dunes, the heat,
the proud libido of the local kids
and all this wine could put you in the mood.

Or we could fight. Tempers wrecked by craters
on the coast road, all this wine and heat,
the cruel machismo of the local kids.

A playful soldier lets you hold his pike,
and poses for the usual photograph.
A voice assails you as you cross the beach

My orders are that towels will be returned.
The shell you find and press against my ear
is intricate and quiet and unexploded.

Cape Cross

At Cape Cross, in Namibia,
a million fur-clad seals converge to breed.

I am watching bodies everywhere
from touching close,
sprawled across the beach so I can barely see the sand,
right out to small black dots bobbing in the distant
froth-breathed breakers and beyond.
Some old large males, too fat for this terrain,
are dragging themselves clumsily across the rocks,
balancing unsteadily.
The tetchy young ones jab at one another,
too lazy to do damage,
posturing aggression, bearing teeth.
Then the females, stretching out upon their supple backs,
exposing doughy, bulbous skin and darker upturned nipples.
And the babies – stumbling nervously, then flopping on the ground.
And the noise – everybody barking, screaming.

At Cape Cross, in Namibia,
a million fur-clad seals converge to breed.
Yes, I shall go there next year,
pleasant though this Spanish island is.

Shark (Juvenile)

Abandoned shoreline hugger, shallows hoodlum,
all questions and insinuating curves,
skin taut as shined, black leather boots,
miniature fin brandished like broken glass.

He acts like he's hanging tough. In fact, he is hiding,
picking on someone who's certainly not his own size,
projecting his future on others' impressionable features.
I'd pull him up now by his dorsal –
   if not for that eye,

that motionless eye, the implicit suggestion of teeth,
the thought of my blood in his water.
                                    He swaggers his tail,
sidles away to continue rehearsing his moves,
is lost in the shadows of all that he has to live up to.

At the Source of the A-Roads

Expecting footprints through a forest glade,
a cattle track that broadens to a path,
a bridleway, a pretty lane, a road?
A grand, grey trunk dual-carriaged from its birth?
The A4 starts at Sainsbury's HQ;
The A2 between Supersave Express,
a bleak hotel, Ryman, Borough Tube,
a 'browse-in' called Galapagos.net.
Their given names are plain – King William Street,
New Fetter Lane and, firstly, Aldersgate
where people dribble through each other's feet
and jostle with their busy London duties,
oblivious to the distances ahead,
of Edinburgh, Dover, Holyhead.

He Contemplates Retirement on the
RMS Queen Mary

I should be decommissioned soon.
      I am creaking. I leak in worrying places.
My heaving bulk just balances
upon the long, unfathomed ocean
and all of my turbulent passages hurt.
I've seemed to hit more troughs than peaks.
      The stewardess who serves my *'first-class luncheon'*
has to hide her sudden yawns
behind her faded soup-soiled cuffs.
      I have outlasted all my glitterati
but still not sunk, so on I sail.

Like you, I was a thing of beauty,
      deserve to be remembered for my glamour.
I too have photographs of actors,
ministers, a plastered Duke,
and someone who might be a model
giggling like an ingénue.
      You have served both actresses and armies.
Me too, in my way, old friend.
Let us both sound our noble horn.
      You remind me, proud outdated boat,
that we must celebrate ourselves.

Let me be becalmed and berthed.
      A monument to everything I meant
to stand for, nothing else admitted.
A little rust can look distinguished.
No vain attempt to reinvent
or overhaul the new designs.
      We've forged our warships into posh hotels.
The porthole view is steady now.
The seagulls circle lazily.
      I'll spend my placid nights reflecting on
the myths I sired, the hearts I won.

26

Ohio

A skeleton smelter – brittle conveyors dusty
with delicate snow. Its final slender flame
vacillates and gusts about its chimney
like a flag. A solitary crane,
drooped as if age has bowed it down,
overhangs the almost-frozen river –
            deep and slow Ohio.

In rust-belt bars, the men who roared across
the mills and stoked the blasting furnaces
have shrivelled into pictures on the walls.
Massage therapists and tattoo artists
sink their Buds with satellite installers
and in-house entertainment engineers
            across Ohio.

The smelter broods like an abandoned dog,
implacable and hostile to the future,
scathing of the young and their machines –
the way they wear their earpieces to gossip,
tap and stroke their flashy little screens,
skate across the ice that's almost melted
            from the deep Ohio.

Wheeling

One time, back in the day, the underground
railway freighted here with fleeing gangs
of slaves as loaded paddle-steamers wound
between the towns that served Ohio's banks.
Their harbours fed the world her glass and steel
and greased her people's passage to the West.
These dirty streets now struggle to seem real –
the theatre's dark, the only hotel closed.
The tourist centre's maps have all been lost.
A truck-man smokes beside his empty load,
kids kick balls between two crumpled posts,
a woman waits to cross a silent road.
Yet these proud dockside houses leave no doubt
that soon enough the tide will turn about.

Hiroshima

Here, your heart can shudder with a camera
flash, the shadow of a circling heron.
A burst of rain exploding on your neck
can wrench your fragile face towards the heavens.
The wrong sort of cloud can leave you breathless.

It's far too much. This narrative where everybody
dies at once, or some days later,
or after years of pain, but in the end.
Museums' stencilled walls assert that next time
there'd be nothing left to resurrect,

and yet the sun is pleasant, warm and honest,
the flirty schoolgirls, girly and flirtatious,
commuters busy and intense. A tourist
leaflet warns *Be careful on our roads.*
Please enjoy the nightlife while you're here.

Borneo

I watch two shy orang-utans make love,
delicate and serious and slow.
I see the flying squirrels don their childish
Batmen capes and glide across the treeline
like balloons. I hear the Buffy Fish Owl's
sudden screech, flinch back into a bush
and touch, it's like a sharp inoculation,
tiger leeches slitting up my skin.
I smell the fertile Kinabatagan
and taste the salty flow of my quick sweat.
Now I am a crested serpent eagle
focused on the moment of attack.
I harden my fixed gaze and scan my depths,
then plunge upon a predetermined kill.

The Final Call

The glockenspiel drone of the public address,
the klaxon of the buggy as it scuttles
to a standstill, drops its bodies off,
picks its way between the sleeping corpses,

those corralled amongst their luggage for protection,
those vulnerably alone,
slowly shedding outer garments,
faces stuffed grotesquely into soiled, makeshift pillows.

Line by line the screens are going blank –
one number and one mocking destination,
one winking blood-red legend:
Vuelo Retrasado. Espere la información.

Rain dribbles through the never-finished roof,
sheets across the sky, the empty tarmac.
Then the air-conditioning expires,
the travelators stop.

Women stare distractedly
at vouchers for a restaurant that has shut.
The men brandish boarding cards and passports
like trumps in a trick they've long since lost.

The gate attendants cluck to one another.
If approached they might dispense a careless shrug.
They know little of our language but can say
There is no information you can have.

The Internationale

On peut regarder le football içi?
Bien sûr, monsieur. The minaret
calls faithful men to prayer; I face the screen.

Slovenia, I don't know? Is she new?
Algeria is disciplined and clean.
You're English? You'll admire our four-four-two.

The Arabic for 'get your arse onside'
seems half-enchantment, half a call to arms.
An imam passes; Belhadj volleys wide.

The couscous comes in jabulani bowls.
I smoke a shisha with a dry Ghanaian.
We share the same beliefs – the game needs goals.

Six South Koreans searching for their match
slip inside and settle for a corner.
A keeper makes a sharp, decisive, catch.

The children butterfly about the streets
in Messi kits; the scattered women set
like brilliants in bright Brazilian shirts.

Love in the Time of Cantona

It's a cruel wind that blows through Rotherham
or Preston of a Saturday. White scarves
fluttering like flags. Muffled chants

through undigested pies. A man cries out –
large of heart and stomach, short of hair,
a veteran of these godless lower leagues.

His shivering fingers spill an off-peak ticket,
dog-eared programme, bobble hat that reads
Champions of 1992.

Once he had a gorgeous, slim brunette
whose blinding smile and rippling effervescence
left him breathless. Then she left.

He gets along. But, oh, those legs, those breasts,
that harsh quicksilver temper and that pleasure.
The game goes on. He thinks he knows the score.

Witness

No-one thanks you for your efforts.
Picture this: an ample mother
stretching out her forearms like
a pelican (replete and fishful)
calmly dries its heavy wings,
then drawing to her fleshy core
one snivelling male infant – snot-flecked
face as crumpled as the paper
bag a refuelled lush discards –
dripping hard and craving justice.
At her side and burrowing
against her loosening grasp, a female
child, all wide-eyes and haloes.

The thrashing pool they stand beside
settles and, at last, reflects.
'It was an accident' she says.
'You see', she says, 'an accident.
Are you sorry?''Yes. I'm sorry.'
'See. She's sorry. You should now
accept her nice apology.'
I intervene – 'I saw it all.
A vicious raking mid-calf hack.
Rooney did the same thing once.
They caught him on the touchline camera,
banned him for the next three matches.'
But no-one thanks you for your efforts.

Space Tourism – The Budget Guide

I am forty million dollars short
of the forty million dollars needed
for a passage to the Zvedzda Module
on the Roscosmos Soyuz Service.

I choose instead a cliff path and a clear night
to search for the International Space
Station. I have a new application –
keen but easily distracted.

It bleeps excitedly at flocks of light,
a red flash of tail, a rumbling cough –
chains of aircraft on their home descent,
the metronomic pattern of a flight path.

Next, the app strains quizzically towards
a distant hanging glow that rocks and steadies,
intelligently pulses and then waits –
the mast of a superyacht.

Somewhere high above this antique sea
greedy banks of solar cells rotate,
tests in microgravity are run,
a urine funnel toilet hose is used.

A sparkle shimmers from behind a cloud,
merely one of the minor stars.
I sense a sudden rush of heavy wings,
just a seagull or a passing angel.

The Astronomers

I am not a little teapot, and though
eleven-twelfths of all these dark field heaven-
watchers laugh, I share the boy's deep pain.
This six-year-old, now sun-faced in his anger.

We Sagittarians are deadly archers;
enchanting noble centaurs of the skies.
Steve's laser-pointer darts: *There's the handle.*
The spout – here – points towards the Scorpion.

At my school, there were stickers in the cloakroom.
A lion, a bear, a hurricane, a spitfire –
and, for me, a teapot. *Lift him up*
And pour him out – I almost vomit now

and stare into Steve's telescope for focus.
Dead centre, in a perfect silhouette,
the ringed planet gleams. I check
the other end. He must have hung a model.

Nothing. Saturn stays suspended in
the screen, as if he could be deftly handled.
Automatic tracking, Steve informs me,
Made for NASA. I've got nine at home.

Trevor, one eye to a lens, is shouting:
Steve, the thing's exploded and there's one part
flapping in a tail-spin east-south-east.
Silence has descended. A couple take

a short step backwards. A child whispers *Alderon.*
Gravely Steve inspects the skies;
in presidential tones announces, *An*
Unlisted Object. A man starts his car,

a baby hiccups. Trevor's on the phone.
Most likely it's a weather balloon says Steve.
This provokes a hum of disappointment.
Or maybe it's a rocket launch. We brighten.

Trevor turns to us and waits for quiet.
Judging by its speed and its position,
the government believes it is connected
to the new Korean space station.

They won't say any more. We nod together
as if this is just what we expected.
Steve readjusts the lens and talks about
Arcturus. *So far out.* Steve's short. And stout.

The British No. 8

A mismatch in the inter-house mixed doubles.
To your horror, I would partner you.
I barely hit a second-serve in Court.
Your double-fisted backhand pulled me through.

I trembled as we held the cup aloft,
and heard the bold headmaster gravely state
We will see you at Wimbledon some day
and now you are the British No. 8.

We did see you at Wimbledon today.
The match was brief. You did not win a game.
The analysts discuss your future prospects.
She might last longer… if it pours with rain.

I hope to see you smash their condescension –
a passing shot to stun the so-called greats –
but if you should lose everything to love,
you're not alone my British No. 8.

Us Veteran Gods

It started at the rugby club.
I winced along the touchline,
the boy meandered near the ball.
I'd never played. He'd rather not.
The weather froze. The team would lose.
But I could talk a better game than most.

By the spring, the memories had flowered.
My final-second winning tries at
Glasgow Academicals and Wasps.
My zig-zag jinks at Twickenham.
Nothing you could obviously Google,
just a hint of international call-ups,
flashes of ill-discipline that left men scarred for life.

The Special Forces Luncheon Club was harder.
Not so much the flab, the chins –
other elite bodies had relaxed a little too –
more the terminology, the mascots,
the exercise *far worse than anything we faced in combat.*
I was Secret Operations –
our existence still officially denied, *so can't say much.*
I'd gravely nod, and pass the port correctly.

I come here most days now.
At first, I'd no idea how a God would have behaved.
I listened to the others –
the creations and the covenants,
the wraths and the eternal forgivings.
I laid out laws and nobody suspected.
I can scarcely believe what some of these chaps did.

Circle Line

Follow the yellow-black rail. Clickety-clack.
Hiss. Sssssh. Doors burst. The high
pressure people pour. You mind the gap,
grab the strap and find you get carried away.

A schoolboy bounds on board at Tower Hill.
Some student lost in his revision prangs
a double-breasted businessman at Temple.
A father fights his pram at Euston Square.

You're almost too preoccupied to notice
that each of them is you. A platform slows.
This frail old man will also join your carriage.
Unless, of course, you jump off here. And now.

Parting

These days, I barely remember a time before you.
Even in these old, old photographs, you're here;
casual, caressing, shading my face,
or spiky, defiant – together we mean business,
and we meant it.

But time, if it brings anything, brings foresight, self-knowledge.
I can see that you will leave me.
Waking every morning, parts of what we were
are left stranded on the bed to be discarded with the night.
We are less and less together.

Soon, the little that remains won't conceal the growing hardness.
First, close friends and family,
colleagues and then strangers in the street, will notice our charade.
They can empathise or snigger.
That will soon all be over, you'll be gone.

Useless objects from our past life will clutter up our home.
I'll send back the dryer, throw away the comb;
age here alone, accepting gracelessly the fact
that I must baldly face the future
or always wear a hat.

Flashpoint

Please don't approach me with that pleasant smile,
that outstretched arm, that look that's half-expectancy
and half-entitlement. I know your gesture says
'this is all you have to press'
but *I'm no good ...*
                    OK, OK, I'll try

No need to speak more slowly. I understand
you want to hold each other dreamily
in front of Tower Bridge just as it opens;
the river view across St Paul's at sunset
(the shot where you are lifting the cathedral).

Before you do, I know I've failed the moment.
I hand the camera back and quickly turn –
my shrinking form at pains to edit out
the solemn scroll, the sigh, the sad delete,
the hope that someone better passes by.

Lament

I am a full-time artist,
Creating abstract stuff.
To-day I have made money.
To-night I shall make love.

I have followed this vocation
Since the twilight of my youth
A long aesthetic quest
To a universal truth

That all of these endeavours
Will never be enough.
For I always want more money
And I always want more love.

Father of the House

I don't suppose my name means much to you.
No reason why it should; for thirteen years
I was the member for Westhampton East.
They know me well back there. If I'm in Tescos,
like as not, I will be buttonholed for hours
on social housing or the local schools –
though even when I mattered there was not
much I could do, but send a standard letter.
It sometimes did some good. You must know
my daughter, she's a legend on the stump.
Her mother, my first wife, would rally too.
You'd feel your heart vibrate on nights like that.
I liked the London work as well. I was
the Minister for Transport's PPS,
then Opposition Whip, then backbench presence.
The Chancellor would ask me to prepare
his speeches on our exports to the States.
I never missed a chance to do the news.
I wrote the party's policy on oil.
And then Westhampton's boundaries were changed.
It seemed a waste of time to even stand.
I got depressed. A foreign junket helped,
some fancy meals, I once or twice got laid,
the little things that make a life worth living.
You're wondering, of course, what happened next.
Some local work. I teach. I make ends meet.
You must excuse me now. I have some words to say,
as befits the father of the bride.

Family Gatherings

The dead don't change. They're always up one end
and uncomplaining. They appreciate
their eulogies – the ghosted mini send-offs,
kind vignettes. And then they slip away.
But how the living age. The loosening hair
and tightening smiles. A black tie stops a little
further up a stomach; heavy tears
now smudge a thicker make-up; when they kneel
some pray for strength to stand. Then shadow hymns,
almost words that hang on almost tunes,
as memories of school-learned music dim.
All understand they'll meet again here soon.
They leave their flowers, quietly turn their thoughts
to sandwiches, some tea, a single malt.

Hedge Hunter

Banks of tiny jitterbug figures.
Everywhere scoped by his blistering stare,
the shot of blood in his eye,
the stink of new digestion on his breath,
the shake of his head from side to side
just before he pounces on the mouse,
vibrates it once or twice and holds it down.
The straight white cuff with the hard blue link
withdraws, dabs a rivulet of sweat at the collar,
grasps a slug of coffee.
A tongue slips across
two rows of sharp white teeth.
The figures dance.
He settles back to watch.

Warriors

Soon we will have burned or buried them all,
that burdened generation, who *did their bit*
on rations, through the rubble, glancing skywards –
air-raid wardens, night fire marshals, wrens,
platform huddlers, radio disciples.
Now they march discreetly to the archives
with all their jingly Morris Men, their serious
priests' politely spoken eulogies –
these sturdy lives that never made the headlines –
for well turned-out inheritors of scrapbooks,
listeners at austere childhood meals
to censored tales of deserts, beaches, oceans,
polishers of medals – aging too.
They were the many. Now they are the few.

Testing Time

You won't go blind. Your mother need not know.
The Doctor says you must. No magazines.
No hints or tips. A pot too small to piss in
(when this is so much harder). Once you're done
a desperate one-hour race to thrust such seed
as you have salvaged in a face which might
or might not say *Yes, this will just suffice.*
You let your mind be filled with filthy thoughts –
but every sexual failure you have suffered
slithers out and limps across your brain
which soon gives up the ghost and thinks of sport
or politics or food. You must hold firm.
It's not as if you don't know what to do.
And in a gloop of spluttered rage –
there has to be a better way,
who wants a baby anyhow – you've come
to this.

When Men Write About Their Fathers

When my father died, my Mum was very ill in hospital, and so I had to organise the funeral. I chose a special coffin and a polished marble urn. They offered me a notice in the local paper. I booked a full page advert in The Times. We talked of music for the service. I said he liked Bob Dylan. They said what about Bob Dylan. I said I think he's touring in the States, but we could try Joan Baez' agent. Tethered to her life support machine, my mother seemed quite happy with my progress.

They spoke of eulogies. I said I had some parting thoughts to share and that my speech would last about a day. I hired a horse-drawn hearse, a battery of cannon for a 50-gun salute, a marching band, an elephant, a chef. I liaised with the police and arranged to close some roads. I chose a poem by the Poet Laureate and I invited her to read it. My mother, breathing now unaided, seemed content.

I knew that once, at a corporate event, my father flew a Hurricane for half an hour. I booked a fly-past. I remembered the day that he had bought a book on yachts. I investigated burial at sea. But then as I sat speaking to my mother of the respective merits of a pyramid and an equestrian statue in the Royal Parks, her eyes flickered open, flushed with anguish, and through a terrible upsurge of pain, she gasped, *Your father, son, never rode a horse.*

50 Black Books

Hard-bound, the year picked out in gold,
Smythson of Bond Street etched across each spine.

Eighteen thousand days, each measuring
one block of crisp white space.

Thirty years ago – a Friday –
11 Mr Jones 2pm Mrs Capstock-Price

Four decades back – *5 o'c*
Pick up kids from Carol's

I find my birth – the week before you'd *test drive car,*
after the home insurance was renewed.

Your mother's funeral, nestled in between
John Lewis sale and *badminton/ lunch with Steve.*

No commentary, just here and there, an exclamation mark!
Double underlining, an ellipsis …

Diagnosis Day, New York

Everything is other in these topsy jet-lagged hours.
Half-past three and noticing the blocks of black,

the yellow glare of early cars, their quick red tails,
the feline green of long alarm-clock stares.

Half-comatose by tea-time,
nodding like a windscreen dog

at every circling skater,
the drop of each quiet leaf,

the bloodshot sunset hung from Bryant Park.
When skaters fall, it jerks me like a halter

back to this Thanksgiving Eve –
crashing into other peoples'

festivals, their different names for seasons.
I check my phone. You haven't called.

I'm waiting for your news
in someone else's city.

Hotspur

I

My father is my age. I am 10 years old.
A birthday treat, a trip to White Hart Lane.
We dribble through the matchday London traffic.
My heart is spreading like my streaming scarf.
We park the car and he unscrews a flask,
pours tea, gives me a chicken sandwich.
We listen to the team news as we eat,
then join the legions swarming to the ground.
I'm frightened by the fighting and the chants.
He takes my hand and gently shunts me forward
until the turnstile clickers shut behind us,
a thousand wooden steps and we emerge.
The players are the size of plastic soldiers.
The pitch is just a doormat someone's painted.
Come on you Spurs. Come on you Lilywhites.

II

Mabbutt, Roberts, Miller, Hughton, Price.
Strong, no-nonsense, one-club sort of men.
A ghostly figure pirouettes alone,
his brief caress unfurls a perfect pass.
Hoddle, Hazard, Perryman, Ardiles
float upfield and flurry round the goal.
Now shaggy Stevie Archibald is leaping.
He heads the ball against the post and in.
The crowd erupts along its coloured fault lines.
My father dives in front to save my hat.

A Full Retirement

Always family came first for him,
doting on his difficult parents, bringing
up the children when his wife passed away.
He worked hard too, the trusted Head of Research
at the aerospace facility

and gave so much to charity, Chair
of trustee boards and Visitor to prisons,
though, in his quieter moments, how he loved
his Art – such understated watercolours,
pastorals flecked with poets, shepherds, sheep.

He retired, and the children all moved out.
He made way for a slightly younger trustee
and chuckled, *Now I've too much time to paint.*
I've space for myself, my health, he said,
but less than two months later he was dead.

Upon the Reuniting

I tilt my glass and straighten up my name badge.
Then I take the plunge,

pitched against the buttoned suits, power-
blouses, taut ties, and slim-fit blazers.

It's warmer once I'm in and babbling through
the shallow lanes of cricket, bikes and Britpop,

fake IDs with violent haircuts, paper
rounds, unhealthy jobs for cash-in-hand.

The drinks begin to overlap like years,
the evening slowly growing even darker.

Where is my career in astrophysics?
My seven children with three different women?

I have not survived an ambush in
Helmand or *crept* toward a cure for cancer.

Instead, I'm telling somebody I only half-
remember how I once went to Peru

and hearing how she dislikes guinea-pigs
but *one time bought a hamster for the children.*

At the death, I hold a heavy whisky
and a listless conversation. Here's

a girl who's *doing something useful with
her life* and a boy who doesn't care.

Meeting the Surrogate

I've hired people to do things for me before.
Wiring up the outside lighting,
installing and retuning the satellite TV,
plumbing in the washer-dryer
and (to my father's shame)
driving.
Or things I could but didn't want to do.
Mowing the lawn,
filling out my tax return,
and (to my mother's shame)
ironing.
But this was different.

I've often met new people –
at weddings, christenings, funerals,
at barbecues, on holiday,
(once) on the tube;
at corporate events,
champagne glass and vol-au-vent in hand,
mindful of my training, 'Maximise Your Networking';
at parties,
friends of friends,
their colleagues, cousins, lovers,
Now, let me introduce you to ...
(my name escapes like bubbles up my glass).
But this was different.

We talked of things anyone might talk of –
the weather in Ohio,
our hopes for the Olympic summer,
the price of peanut jelly,
No, I haven't met the Queen.
I once saw David Beckham in a bar –
and things that they might not.

Our repeated miscarriages and desperate prognoses.
Her pair of
vaginal deliveries,
her faith in God,
how she knew that Jesus wanted her to help us in this way.
Yes, this was different.

The Introduction

It's always the same with valuable people. They bugger
up your schedule. Years of trying – hopeful
we might meet, then sudden disappointment.
I'd made sure I'd be back for your arrival

and then I got the call that you'd come early,
guessed that you'd be seeing other people, networking
around. I bribed my way on board the soonest
plane, bagged half the airport gift shop, bounced

across the pond, charged through customs, jumped
a seething taxi queue, screeched into
a murmuring reception, drowsy lift,
a dozen endless corridors. A room.

And there you were. Staring, saying nothing.
Should I have shook your hand or bowed? Instead,
I held you in my arms. Delicate
and curious and three-days old.

Born in the USA

Sometimes red and red make blue.
Your new world birth-right proven here
by one gymnastic eagle, meaty
Presidential quotes, arresting frontier images.
They echo Her Britannic Majesty's
demand that you pass freely without hindrance,
afforded all protection you may need.
I turn to your miraculous photographs –
no smiles, no parents' hands, and no shut eyes.
Your bemused-to-be-here stare took seven hours
to capture. Six weeks later you're already
someone else for border guards to puzzle.
Four passports nest across my span –
a magic trick, an improbably fortunate hand.

[   ]

Much of the moon
is squinting at me,
supported by stars
I can't name any more.

I forget
the moon will wax and wane.
Does it not blossom, ripen,
then switch like a lamp?

I right myself and then I can't recall
the name of the last Pope,
the shadow foreign secretary,
the capital of Chile.

This often happens –
I used to thrash my mind
as ocean-beaten swimmers
smash the waves and gasp.

Now I let the absences wash over,
tides caressing through the rock pools.
The inrush brings deposits,
things are lost in the receding.

I'm soothed by every motion, gently murmur
Benedictus, Alexander, Santiago,
as I forget
the title of this poem.

A Passiontide Christening

The organ clears its throat and people stand.
Clergy process down the aisle in pairs –
canons who this week squirmed awkwardly
on different sides of what the BBC describes
as *homosexual marriage issues.*
The canon on the right will lead the prayers.
He calls for blessings on our righteous Queen
and parliament and God's own timeless laws,

but several hundred eyes are not quite focused
on the lectern. They are watching as I
wrestle with my daughter, a milky-fingered
father and a baby dribbling down
a lacy front while scattering an ark
of sudden animals. The Missioner retrieves
a meerkat from the retrochoir.
Then the action switches to the font –

the candidates for baptism have gathered.
My daughter defecates discreetly.
The thurifer oscillates the censer
like a campanologist on steroids.
The holy smoke disperses some relief.
As quickly as he can, the canon-pastor
dunks the baby, mumbles, hands her back.
He'll mark the start of the Triduum

by washing people's feet. He does not change
their babies. We hear the Gospel of St. John.
The canon on the left will preach the sermon.
The reading we have heard today is timely,
reminds us all that we are who He made us,
our sexuality's a gift from God –
my baby claps her hands and starts to shout -
as *'Jesus said to Lazarus: Come Out'.*

Care and Attention

She likes to draw blood
with a sharp red pencil,

deeply etched, repeated scratches.
She talks intently to her insects,

Hello Ant; will spend an afternoon
transferring her seashells

from a bucket to another bucket.
I've learned to catch a change of smell,

a sudden squall, whilst web-combing the news sites,
digging through an avalanche of emails.

A post, a tweet, a brief Reply to All
while one hand spoons the sweetcorn,

smears the bruise. A showering of facts,
like the scatter of a hundred pencils,

which she will gather and re-order
by reference to her colour chart.

'tell me the lowest line you can clearly read'

H

OME

CAREER

FAMILYCRISES

PERSONALFINANCES

LOCALCOMMUNITYISSUES

KEYNEWPOLITICALTHOUGHT

RELIGIOUSTRUTHLONGTERMMACROEC

ONOMICLANDSCAPESTHEFUTUREOFTHENATIO

NSTATETHETIMEANDMANNEROFYOUROWNENCROACHINGDEATH